# Gourmet Grub: Fondue!

From Cheese to Chocolate, The Best Fondue Recipes for All Occasions

BY

Stephanie Sharp

Copyright © 2019 by Stephanie Sharp

## Copyright 2019 by Stephanie Sharp

All rights reserved.

No part of this publication may be reproduced, stored in a retrieval system, stored in a database and / or published in any form or by any means, electronic, mechanical, photocopying, recording or otherwise, without the prior written permission of the publisher.

## Warning - Disclaimer

The purpose of this book is to educate and entertain. The author and does not guarantee that anyone following these techniques, suggestions, tips, ideas, or strategies will become successful. The author shall have neither liability nor responsibility to anyone with respect to any loss or damage caused, or alleged to be caused, directly or indirectly by the information contained in this book.

Thank you so much for purchasing my book! As a reward for your purchase, you can now receive free books sent to you every day. All you have to do is just subscribe to the list by entering your email address in the box below and I will send you a notification every time I have a free promotion running. The books will absolutely be free with no work at all from you! Who doesn't want free books? No one! There are free and discounted books every day, and an email is sent to you 1-2 days beforehand to remind you so you don't miss out. It's that easy!

*Just visit the link or scan QR-code to get started!*

https://stephanie-sharp.subscribemenow.com

# Table of Contents

Introduction .................................................................. 9

From A Peasant Dish to A Special Treat: Fondue's History Revealed ..................................................................... 12

The Official National Dish of Switzerland ....................... 13

Fondue Invades America .................................................. 15

The French Fondue ........................................................... 17

The Asian Fondue (Hotpot) .............................................. 18

Fondue Party Hosting 101 ................................................ 19

Planning your Party .......................................................... 20

Set Up the Table ............................................................... 22

Bring in a Good Quality Wine ......................................... 23

Fondue Etiquette ............................................................... 24

Get Ready to Fondue ........................................................ 27

The Fondue Pot ................................................................. 28

Other Tools ............................................................................ 30

Food for Dipping.................................................................. 32

Fondue Tips and Tricks ....................................................... 34

    Swiss Cheese Fondue ..................................................... 37

    Classic Meat Fondue ....................................................... 40

    Cheesy Squash Fondue................................................... 42

    Italian-Style Pancetta Fondue......................................... 45

    Shrimps and Scallops Fondue ........................................ 48

    Beer-Cheese Fondue ....................................................... 51

    Pesto Fondue .................................................................. 54

    Onion Fondue.................................................................. 57

    Crab Fondue .................................................................... 60

    Roasted Garlic Broth ....................................................... 63

    Spanish-Style Fondue...................................................... 66

    Greek Fondue .................................................................. 68

Smoky Mozzarella Fondue ... 71

Fiery Cheddar Fondue ... 74

Brie and Maple Syrup Fondue ... 76

Pizza Fondue ... 79

Mexican-Style Fondue ... 81

Spiced Oil Fondue ... 83

Chinese Hot Pot ... 85

Swiss Tomato Fondue ... 88

Quick & Easy Chocolate Fondue ... 90

Creamy Matcha Fondue ... 92

Chocolate Cheesecake Fondue ... 94

Caramel Fondue ... 96

Red Velvet Fondue ... 98

Cinnamon Roll Fondue ... 100

S'mores Fondue ... 102

Butterscotch Fondue ................................................... 104

Lemon Fondue .......................................................... 106

Mocha Fondue .......................................................... 108

Conclusion ................................................................ 110

# Introduction

A fondue pot steaming with something appetizing, waiting for a morsel of food to be dipped in, seems like a very simple dish. But there's more to the fondue than meets the eye. It's more than just a dip. It's a masterpiece that have made its way from the simple pots used in the 17th century Switzerland to the modern day fondue pots, which readily come with a heating element and utensils.

The fondue also grew steadily from the simple savory cheese to sweet and tangy and other flavor mixes. Indeed, it has exceeded expectations by becoming a phenomenon, a craze, a cuisine in its own right.

If you want to get started in concocting your own fondue mixes, this is the right cookbook for you. We gathered the best and tastiest recipes that will give you a head start on putting together a fondue party. They are also perfect for making impressive snacks that both kids and adults would love. We promise that you will reign supreme in your kitchen anew by perusing this luscious lineup:

- Swiss Cheese Fondue
- Classic Meat Fondue
- Cheesy Squash Fondue
- Italian-Style Pancetta Fondue
- Shrimps and Scallops Fondue
- Beer-Cheese Fondue
- Pesto Fondue
- French Onion Fondue
- Crab Fondue
- Roasted Garlic Broth
- Spanish-Style Fondue
- Greek Fondue
- Smokey Mozzarella Fondue
- Fiery Cheddar Fondue
- Brie and Maple Syrup Fondue
- Pizza Fondue

- Mexican-Style Fondue
- Spiced Oil Fondue
- Chinese Hotpot
- Swiss Tomato Fondue
- Quick & Easy Chocolate Fondue
- Creamy Matcha Fondue
- Chocolate Cheesecake Fondue
- Caramel Fondue
- Red Velvet Fondue
- Cinnamon Roll Fondue
- S'mores Fondue
- Butterscotch Fondue
- Lemon Fondue
- Mocha Fondue

# From A Peasant Dish to A Special Treat: Fondue's History Revealed

The fondue that we now know is a far cry from what it was originally.

Fondue was first introduced in the Valais region of Switzerland during the 17th Century. It was a peasant dish, intended to allow the locals make use of their abundant supply of cheese, bread, and wine. They use those aged supplies so people who do not have access to fresh produce, especially during winter time, would have something to eat.

The term "fondue" was from a French word "fondre", which means "to melt". That French part of the history of fondue is due to the fact that the Valais region is a French canton.

# The Official National Dish of Switzerland

Fast forward to the 1930s, fondue was not only widely consumed all over Switzerland but was also declared as the official national dish by the Swiss Cheese Union. This was to make sure the nation would increase its cheese consumption to make use of the available supplies.

The Swiss Cheese Union, an alliance of cheese producers in Switzerland, might have collapsed in the late 1990s but the mark that the fondue made in the global market is definitely to stay. In fact, it has even spread, inspiring other cuisines to develop their own unique fondue recipes, – from the sweet chocolate to the savory meat broth and everything else in between.

# Fondue Invades America

The US version of the fondue, which is made of chocolate instead of cheese, best characterizes the Americans' sweet tooth and their love for dessert. So, how did it happen?

It all started in the 1964 New York World's Fair, where the Americans first noticed the Swiss fondue. In no time, they were able to present a sweet food fad that has spread like a wild fire. From there, the fondue found its way as a dinner party element, a must have for an even more exciting buffet spread.

# The French Fondue

As per France, they are much into a loaded meat fondue than anything else. The early origins of this dish are traced back to the vineyards of Burgundy. The workers have found the idea of keeping a boiling pot of oil burning because it allows them for a quick meal whenever they get an opportunity to take a break. The French fondue is also known as Fondue Bourguignonne.

# The Asian Fondue (Hotpot)

Meanwhile, in Asia, the fondue pot is made bigger, into a hotpot. This is where they brew a delicious broth and dip in different food morsels. It's a lighter version of the French's meat fondue but it's equally satisfying.

There might be a hundred ways to make a fondue nowadays, from one part of the world to another, but this thing remains constant: it's a communal dining experience meant to be shared.

# Fondue Party Hosting 101

In Switzerland, where fondue originated, and practically everywhere else in the world, the fondue is used as a party centerpiece. It's that communal bowl everyone is looking forward to dig into. Depending on your recipe or your occasion, the fondue can be served as an appetizer, main course meal, or even as a dessert. That's how versatile the dish is.

It is not at all surprising that people go out of their way to host a fondue party. Imagine, a shindig that goes around a fondue pot?

# Planning your Party

Just like with any party, you have to plan your fondue party carefully. Setting up the menu has so much to do with the number of guests that you expect to arrive and the venue in which you are holding the party.

Consider a theme and plan your music, entertainment, décor, and even food choices around it. You must stay true to your theme to make it truly impressive.

Also, for a fondue party to work, you must have the proper equipment ready. Depending on how many fondue variants you plan to prepare and the how big your group is, you will need a couple of fondue pots together with forks. You must also have a couple of serving trays in which you will lay you're your dipping ingredients, which may range from bread to meat pieces or seafood, fruits, marshmallows or cookies, and everything else in between. You need to have as many trays as you can prepare because some dipping ingredients should not be placed side by side due to contamination. Otherwise, you can choose party trays with dividers. They are both functional and appealing.

Then, you should plan the perfect fondue recipe to prepare. You can make anything from the basic cheese fondue to extravagant recipes with bits and pieces. Plus, you can add up a chocolate fondue, which is always a scene-stealer.

# Set Up the Table

You can never go wrong as long as you have a fondue, plus several trays of various bite-size food pieces. The only thing you need to mind is how to decorate the table with an eyecatching centerpiece. If you are hosting for a small group, you can simply place the fondue pot/s at the center of the table, then, the dipping ingredients surrounding them. Taking the time to make sure everything is accessible to everyone, that everyone can indulge.

# Bring in a Good Quality Wine

No fondue party is ever complete without a wine. Make sure it's worth the indulgence. The quality of your wine can make or break the party so be sure to bring in one that will keep everyone satisfied.

There's not much fuss putting together a fondue party. It's just like any ordinary party, only, the fondue is the centerpiece.

# Fondue Etiquette

In its most authentic form, a fondue is a group activity. It's a masterpiece placed at the center of the dining table so everyone will have access to it, can reach in, and get their food morsel dipped into the delightful concoction. It's a communal experience that's meant to be shared with your friends and family. That said, there are dining etiquette that were developed about the fondue.

In Switzerland, people are made to make "the pledge", which means you are going to perform a consequence or a bet if you fumbled with your bread and lose it on the fondue.

The consequence could be anything from simple to something really cheeky. But that's just meant for fun. A fondue after all, is a playful meal for a group of friends or family members hanging out. That said, there are still a couple of rules to go by so you don't turn off the other diners:

- Strictly no double dipping. Do not re-dip your food once you have taken a bite.
- The food morsel must also be removed from the fondue fork by the front teeth. Make sure your lips and your tongue do not touch the tines of the fork.
- For the most part, each diner is provided individual plates and forks. After dipping food onto the communal bowl using the fondue fork, you can slide the food on the plate to let the fondue drip onto it before eating it with your own dinner fork.
- When partaking on a cheese fondue, it has been a tradition that you start with bread. Well, it makes sense. A crusty bread offers a great base that will prepare your stomach for everything else, especially if you are having wine with your fondue.
- Always use a fondue fork to dip the food onto the communal bowl. Never use your fingers or your very own dinner fork. It I also considered unethical to scoop cheese out of the bowl and onto your plate.

It may seem like there are just too many rules of etiquette surrounding the fondue. If you don't want to get dirty looks of disappointment, you would be careful, especially when you are sharing the fondue pot with Swiss nationals who take the meal as seriously as an integral part of their culture. Then again, that should never keep you from enjoying dunking in food morsels on a delightful pot and onto your stomach.

# Get Ready to Fondue

Fondue making has become quite popular not just in Switzerland but in other parts of the world as well. It makes for a great buffet centerpiece, keeping the table colorful with a variety of dipping ingredients, plus the presence of an elegant fondue pot. Before you fondue, however, you must be ready with the right gear.

# The Fondue Pot

The first thing that you must invest in is a good quality pot that is perfect for melting your cheese, chocolate, or any fondue ingredient that you pick – and keeping it warm. There are a lot of different pots available in the market, made of either ceramic, metal, or cast iron material.

A ceramic pot is considered most useful if you are preparing cheese and chocolate fondues that do not require too much heat. When all you need is keeping the dipping sauce warm in low heat, this is a good choice for you.

A metal pot, on the other hand, is for those fondue recipes that require high heat. Meat broths and seafood sauces are most suitable for this because they can keep the fondue in a rolling boil. Alternately, you may use the metal fondue pot for your cheeses and chocolates, as long as you can control the heat source and keep it low.

The cast iron fondue pot, which usually has an enamel finish, is highly preferred because it is pretty versatile. You can use it with any type of fondue recipe, plus, it looks very appealing when placed at the center of the table.

But you don't really have to cook the fondue on the pot. It may sometimes take a good amount of time doing that. For the most part, a fondue set is bought for presentation purposes. You can always cook the fondue in a pressure cooker or a regular stove-top pan, as per the requirement of your recipe.

# Other Tools

It takes more than just a fondue pot to host a party for a number of guests. You also have to prepare the following (if they did not come ready with the pot you bought):

- A heating source. Fondues are served either steaming hot or just warm enough. For that, you need a heating element. It could come from anything – either a built-in electric heat source, gel fuel, candle, or liquid fuel.

- Fondue forks. Long and sleek and pointed, these forks usually come with fondue pots. They are used for dipping the food and not for consuming it. They are color coded so diners will be able to identify their own fork, which they must stick to according to the fondue etiquette.
- Individual plates. While you share the communal bowl or fondue pot, you must never eat straight from it. That's why individual plates are provided to each of the diner present.
- Dinner forks. Just like with plates, diners are provided their own set of utensils so they won't be eating straight from the communal bowl, which is of course, considered bad manners.
- Table napkins. Eating fondue can be pretty messy, especially for those who are first timers. It is best, therefore, that you have table napkins ready.

# Food for Dipping

When the pot and the utensils are all set, there's only the fondue and the dipping ingredients left for you to think about. Since we are tackling the different fondue variants on the recipe section, we will just give you some delectable ideas for the dipping ingredients, cut into bite-size pieces, either sliced into cubes or wedges if they are not yet. Check out this list?

- Crusty breads like French bread, Italian bread, and rye bread.
- Meats like chicken, salami, ham, sausage, beef, pork, meatballs, and seafood.
- Firm fruits like bananas, apples, strawberries, mangoes, kiwis, cherries, peaches, oranges, and grapes.
- Dried or pickled fruits and others.
- Vegetables like potatoes, cauliflower, broccoli, turnips, squash, corn on the cob, onions, and mushrooms.
- Cakes, vanilla cookies, marshmallows, brownies, pretzels, crackers, granola bars, and muffins.
- Other food bits that you will love dipping into fondue include tortilla chips and cheeses.

# Fondue Tips and Tricks

Fondue recipes are widely varied. You have endless choices of what to make in your fondue pot and what dipping ingredients to prepare. You can even arrange different sauce accompaniments as needed. You practically have an upper hand on making the fondue experience a memorable and gastronomically pleasurable for everyone. To help you make everything perfect, take a cue from the following tips:

- Never leave out the crust that forms at the bottom of a cheese fondue. In Switzerland, it is called "la religuese" la croute". It is considered a delicacy that is scraped off the pan and served to guests.
- Trim and slice meats before serving. You can even coat it in marinade. If you are dipping meats in a low temp fondue such as a cheese fondue, it is advisable that you precook the meat.
- Give your prepared fruits and vegetables a good squeeze of lemon juice to keep their bright color.
- Prepare raw meats in separate trays so they will not contaminate the other ingredients. Keep them meats chilled in the fridge until you are ready.
- Pat dry meat and vegetables so they will not create dangerous spatters once dipped into hot fondue.
- Meat broths must be consistent with the meat choice: beef on beef broth; chicken on chicken broth.
- Keep a close watch on your fondue pot, especially if it is extremely hot and if children are around.
- The amount of time you must keep your food ingredient dipped onto fondue depends on the type of food you are dipping and the temperature to which you are dipping it in.

- Never use fresh breads or freshly made cakes. They must be at least one-day-old. One-day-old breads and cakes are firm and will not crumble when dipped into fondue.
- Keep fruits chilled before dipping to make sure the sauce stick.
- The ideal proportion is for only about 4 people sharing a fondue pot. If you are hosting a party for more than 4, you have to invest on several pots.
- If hosting a fondue party, make sure that you choose what course you will assign the fondue. Never serve it as an appetizer, main course meal, and dessert all at once.
- Keep the fondue pot only one-thirds full. This is to avoid spattering when people starts to dip their food.
- To decide on how much food to prepare for your guests, the rule of thumb is half a pound of food for each person, given that you are serving other entrées as well.

You are so ready to fondue! Let's start!

# Swiss Cheese Fondue

There's no better way to start this fondue cookbook than with this traditional Swiss cheese fondue. It's a combination of three different and delectable Swiss cheeses: Gruyere, Raclette, and Emmental. The original recipe calls for wine but if you want to make your fondue alcohol-free, you may substitute with apple cider vinegar. This Swiss cheese fondue makes for a great start at a fondue party, especially when served together with crusty French bread slices and a couple of pickled vegetables. Let's start with this and the let the fondue fun begins.

**Serving Size:** 10

**Prep Time:** 15 mins

**Ingredients:**

- 8oz Gruyere cheese, grated
- 8oz Raclette cheese, grated
- 8oz Emmental cheese, grated
- 1 ½ cups dry white wine
- 2 tbsp lemon juice
- 2 tbsp cornstarch
- 1 garlic clove, halved crosswise
- Pinch of nutmeg
- Pinch of white pepper
- 1 pc French bread loaf, cut into cubes
- 3 cups assorted pickled vegetables

**Instructions:**

1. Heat wine in a pan on low.

2. Gradually add the cheeses when the liquid starts to get bubbly, stirring continuously until completely melted.

3. Combine lemon juice and cornstarch in a bowl until blended.

4. Pour mixture onto fondue, stirring until smooth and bubbly.

5. Season with nutmeg and pepper. Remove from heat.

6. Rub garlic on the insides of your fondue pot. Discard the garlic.

7. Pour cheese fondue on prepared pot, keeping the warmer on low.

8. Place French bread cubes and assorted pickled vegetables in serving platters.

9. Serve with the cheese fondue.

# Classic Meat Fondue

The real secret to a successful meat fondue party is on the dipping sauces, really. It is best that you prepare a handful of choices so your guests could decide for themselves whether to go for sweet, tangy, salty, spicy, or any taste they might prefer. That said, you must not take for granted how delightfully prepared the fondue itself must be. Plus, make sure that the meat is super fresh. You can never go wrong with that.

**Serving Size:** 4

**Prep Time:** 30 mins

**Ingredients:**

- 2 lbs. beef tenderloin, sliced into 1-inch strips
- 1 L vegetable oil
- 1 cup crusty white bread, sliced
- 2 cups green salad

**Instructions:**

1. Fill the fondue pot halfway through with oil.

2. Light the heating element on medium and keep the oil temperature at around 375 degrees F.

3. Place meat and bread in different serving plates together with small bowls of different sauces.

4. Provide your guests with a fondue fork each and let them dunk their meat onto hot oil.

# Cheesy Squash Fondue

Some cheesy goodness works well with the slightly sweet taste of squash. It feels like heaven in your mouth, especially when you dunk it spinach and artichokes into the mix. Imagine the gooey cheese texture made flavorful with squash and bits of chunky goodness from spinach and artichoke? Sounds appetizing, right?

**Serving Size:** 4

**Prep Time:** 1 hr. 25 mins

**Ingredients:**

- 2 cups Gruyere cheese, freshly grated
- 2oz Neufchatel cheese
- 2 pcs acorn squash, halved crosswise and seeds removed
- 4oz fresh spinach, chopped
- 7oz artichoke hearts, drained
- 2 tbsp butter
- 1 cup half-and-half
- Salt and pepper to taste
- 1 pc baguette loaf, sliced

**Instructions:**

1. Preheat the oven to 400 degrees F. Prepare a baking dish lined with foil.

2. Arrange squash halves onto prepared pan. Sprinkle some salt and pepper. Set aside.

3. Melt butter in a pan over medium fire and sauté chopped spinach until slightly wilted.

4. Add artichoke hearts and continue sautéing for 3 minutes more.

5. Transfer mixture to a bowl and mix together with half-and-half, plus Neufchatel cheese until blended.

6. Scoop onto squash halves, keeping them ¾ full.

7. Cover top with grated Gruyere cheese.

8. Place a sheet of aluminum foil on the baking pan to cover the squash. Bake in preheated oven for an hour.

9. After an hour, remove foil, turn up the temperature, and cook for another 5 minutes, until top is brown and the cheese is bubbly.

10. Serve cheesy squash fondue in separate plates with sliced baguette.

# Italian-Style Pancetta Fondue

The flavors of Italy ideally come together for this rich cheese fondue made of Gruyere and Fontina cheese, plus some chopped pancetta for a chunky bite. This is the perfect dipping sauce for Focaccia bread as well as plain-tasting vegetables like radish. What are you waiting for? Let's get down and do this!

**Serving Size:** 4

**Prep Time:** 30 mins

**Ingredients:**

- 1 cup Fontina cheese, grated
- 1 cup Gruyere cheese, grated
- 4oz pancetta, chopped
- 1 ½ cups dry white wine
- 2 tbsp all-purpose flour
- 1 tsp chives, chopped
- 1 pc Focaccia bread loaf, sliced into cubes
- 2 cup radish, trimmed and sliced

**Instructions:**

1. Combine cheeses and flour in a bowl and set aside.

2. Meanwhile, brown chopped pancetta in a pan over medium fire for about 10 minutes or until crisp. Transfer in a bowl and set aside, discarding rendered fat.

3. In the same pan, simmer dry white wine.

4. Gradually add cheese mix and stir constantly until melted and blended.

5. Stir in cooked pancetta, garnish with chopped chives, and serve on a fondue pot over low heat with sliced focaccia bread and radishes.

# Shrimps and Scallops Fondue

A decadent fondue loaded with seafood is definitely irresistible. It's a perfect dinner date idea for couples who just want to spend time together over a light but very filling meal coupled with a good glass of wine. What's even more exciting with this dish is that, you don't have to stick to just shrimps and scallops. You may add in a few seafood choices as well, including crabmeat, lobster, or flaked fish. Let your imagination run wild.

**Serving Size:** 4

**Prep Time:** 30 mins

**Ingredients:**

- 1 lb. shrimp, peeled and deveined
- 12oz scallops, chopped
- 16oz Monterey Jack cheese
- 2 cups mushrooms, sliced
- ½ cup green onions, diced
- 2 cups spinach leaves
- 1 ½ cups onion, diced
- 2 tbsp garlic, minced
- 10 tbsp butter, divided
- 1 ½ cups organic white wine
- 1 ½ cups cream
- 6 tbsp flour
- 1 tsp sea salt
- 1 tbsp Cajun seasoning
- 1 pc crusty sourdough, cut into 1-inch cubes

**Instructions:**

1. Melt 2 tablespoons of butter in a pan on high heat.

2. Add shrimps and scallops, sprinkle with salt and Cajun seasoning, and stir for about 5 minutes.

3. Turn heat to medium and add mushrooms, spinach, green onions, and garlic. Continue to stir until spinach is slightly wilted. Transfer to a fondue pot and set aside.

4. Heat remaining butter in the same pan over medium fire and sauté onion for about 2 minutes until translucent.

5. Pour wine and simmer on low heat for about 7 minutes.

6. Whisk in cream and cheeses and season with some salt. Allow cheeses to melt, stirring frequently for about 5 minutes more.

7. Pour fondue onto prepared pot with seafood and veggies, place heat source on low, and stir to blend.

8. Serve with bread cubes.

# Beer-Cheese Fondue

Got a game night to prepare for? Try making this Beer-Cheese Fondue as your meal offer and impress your group. It takes a unique twist on the authentic recipe by adding beer instead of wine into the recipe. It also uses cheddar cheese, which offers a sharp taste, instead of the usual Swiss cheeses. Try the difference and you will love it, most definitely, including your friends. Serve it with crusty bread slices, soft pretzels, and apples as the perfect dippers.

**Serving Size:** 6

**Prep Time:** 20 mins

**Ingredients:**

- 1 cup beer
- 4 cups cheddar cheese, shredded
- 1 pc onion, chopped
- 4 garlic cloves, minced
- 1 tbsp flour
- 1 tbsp butter
- 3 tbsp half-and-half

**Instructions:**

1. Combine cheese and flour in a bowl and set aside.

2. Melt butter in a pan over medium fire and sauté onions and garlic for about 5 minutes or until fragrant.

3. Pour beer and boil, then, turn heat to low and continue cooking on a simmer while gradually adding cheese and flour mixture and stirring to melt.

4. Add half-and-half and transfer to a fondue pot to keep warm.

5. Serve with your choice of dipping ingredients.

# Pesto Fondue

The thing with cheese fondue is that it only has one significant character, that given off by the gooey, rich tasting cheese that was melted to perfection. But different fondue recipes intended to change the perspective towards the qualifying characteristics of a fondue. In this recipe, for example, pesto is added into the equation. It offers a balancing act to the gooey, cheesy concoction. To make the flavors of basil leaves and garlic standout, a milder cheese is required for this dish.

**Serving Size:** 4

**Prep Time:** 15 mins

**Ingredients:**

- 3 cups mozzarella cheese, shredded
- 1 cup Parmesan cheese, shredded
- ½ cup fresh basil leaves, chopped
- 3 cloves garlic, peeled
- ¼ cup almonds, toasted
- 1 ½ cups dry white wine
- 2 tbsp cornstarch
- Pinch of ground black pepper

**Instructions:**

1. Place basil, garlic, and toasted almonds in a food processor. Pulse until smooth, stirring in about ¼ cup of wine in the process.

2. Put pesto mix and the remaining wine in a pan over medium fire. Let it boil, then, turn heat to low.

3. Combine together Parmesan and mozzarella cheeses, together with cornstarch.

4. Gradually add cheese mixture onto the pan, stirring constantly until the cheese has completely melted and the mixture starts to become stringy. Sprinkle with some pepper to taste.

5. Place the pesto fondue in a fondue pot, keeping warm on low heat.

6. Serve with your favorite dipping ingredients.

# Onion Fondue

The French have their own tasty version of the fondue. It is often just oil and meat. They usually keep some flavored oil hot, then, a platter of fresh, properly cut chunks of meat surrounding it. They dip meat chunks onto hot oil, cook it according to the level of doneness they like, and consume it together with a lovely glass of wine. But this French Onion Fondue is different. It features a well-loved recipe and turn it into a dipping concoction.

**Serving Size:** 4

**Prep Time:** 1 hr. 22 mins

**Ingredients:**

- 4 cups Gruyere, shredded
- 5 cups onion, thinly sliced
- 2 tsp fresh thyme, chopped
- ¼ cup dry white wine
- ¾ cup dry sherry
- 1 cup beef broth
- 1 tbsp unsalted butter
- 1 tbsp olive oil
- 1 tbsp cornstarch
- Salt and pepper to taste

**Instructions:**

1. Combine cheese, thyme, and cornstarch in a bowl. Set aside.

2. Heat oil and butter together in a pan over medium fire and sauté the onions until fragrant.

3. Pour in stock and boil, then, reduce heat to low and simmer for 45 minutes or until the onions are browned and the liquid has significantly reduced.

4. Remove onions with a slotted spoon and into a bowl, then, increase heat back to medium.

5. Pour in sherry and wine, deglazing the pan, while scraping the browned bits at the bottom.

6. Gradually add cheese mixture, stirring and melting with every handful.

7. Place back the onions, sprinkle with some salt and pepper, and transfer to a fondue pot to keep warm.

8. Serve with crusty bread slices and other suitable dipping ingredients.

# Crab Fondue

Crabmeat is another ingredient you can blend into fondue. It's an addictive blend that would make for the perfect comfort food, especially during cold winter days. This is a great recipe to prepare, either for a regular family meal or a special Friday night chill-out dinner with friends.

**Serving Size:** 8

**Prep Time:** 30 mins

**Ingredients:**

- 1 lb. crabmeat
- 18oz cream cheese
- 1 tsp Dijon mustard
- 1 tsp lemon zest
- ¼ cup green onion, chopped
- ½ cup mayonnaise
- 2 tbsp powdered sugar
- 1 ½ tsp Old Bay seasoning
- ½ tsp garlic powder
- ½ cup dry white wine
- 2 tsp lemon juice
- 1 pc Italian bread loaf, cut into 1-inch cubes

**Instructions:**

1. Combine cream cheese, mayonnaise, mustard, Old Bay seasoning, garlic powder, powdered sugar, and lemon zest in a double boiler until the cheese is melted and the ingredients are completely melted.

2. Add wine, lemon juice, crabmeat and chopped green onions. Stir to blend.

3. Transfer into a fondue pot on low heat to keep the crab fondue warm and serve with sliced bread.

# Roasted Garlic Broth

If you want a plain broth where you can dunk chunks of meat and vegetables, this is the recipe for you. Enjoy the hearty comfort of this dish, with its subtle garlic taste, which will help the flavors of your dipping ingredients shine. And oh, that remind us, to make you choose your dipping ingredients carefully, keeping it to your favorite chunks for best results.

**Serving Size:** 6

**Prep Time:** 1 hr. 10 mins

**Ingredients:**

- 3 heads garlic, the top part sliced
- 1 pc onion, finely chopped
- ½ cup sherry wine
- 6 cups chicken broth
- 3 tbsp olive oil
- Salt and pepper to taste

**Instructions:**

1. Preheat the oven to 400 degrees F, placing the wire rack on the second level.

2. Place garlic in aluminum foil, drizzle with a tablespoon of oil, and crumple the foil to close.

3. Allow the garlic to roast for 50 minutes or until super tender.

4. Press the garlic to get the puree. Set aside and discard the solids.

5. Heat the remaining 2 tablespoons of oil and sauté the onions until browned.

6. Pour in wine until most of the liquid has evaporated.

7. Whisk in garlic puree and chicken broth, then, boil. Continue cooking in a simmer for about 5 minutes.

8. Season with salt and pepper and stir.

9. Transfer to a fondue pot and keep warm while preparing your dipping ingredients.

# Spanish-Style Fondue

If you are having a tapas night, we have something that you could add into your menu and make your Spanish party even more special. Yes, this fondue will keep the night alive with its energetic flavors, thanks to paprika. It's a very simple dish and requires only a few ingredients that you throw into a crockpot and you can walk away. But the taste is something else. It is pretty layered and truly exciting.

**Serving Size:** 4

**Prep Time:** 1 hr. 30 mins

**Ingredients:**

- 2 cups Gruyere cheese, shredded
- 2 cups Manchego cheese, shredded
- Pinch of smoked paprika
- 1 clove garlic, peeled and halved
- 2 tbsp all-purpose flour
- 1 cup dry white wine
- 1 pc baguette, sliced into cubes
- 1 cup cured chorizo, sliced
- 2 cups apple, sliced

**Instructions:**

1. Throw all the ingredients into a crockpot or slow cooker, except for baguette, chorizo, and apples. Cook on high for an hour and 30 minutes, removing the garlic on the first 15 minutes and stirring the mixture every 20 minutes.

2. Transfer to a fondue pot and serve with baguette, chorizo, and apples in serving platters.

# Greek Fondue

A Greek-style fondue is something that adventurous foodies should try. It is packed with amazing flavors that would keep your mealtime ultra exciting. With chunky tomatoes reigning supreme, this is best consumed with crusty bread slices and chips.

**Serving Size:** 8

**Prep Time:** 35 mins

**Ingredients:**

- 1 cup feta cheese, crumbled
- 1 cup mozzarella cheese, shredded
- 8oz cream cheese, softened
- 1 cup cherry tomatoes, halved
- ½ cup kalamata olives, sliced
- 2 garlic cloves, minced
- 1 tbsp parsley, chopped
- 1 ¼ tbsp dill, chopped
- 1 tsp lemon zest
- ¼ tsp red pepper flakes
- 1/3 cup Greek yogurt
- ¼ cup whole milk
- 2 tbsp lemon juice
- 2 tbsp olive oil
- Kosher salt and black pepper to taste
- 2 cups pita chips

**Instructions:**

1. Heat a tablespoon of oil in a pan over medium fire and sauté garlic for a minute.

2. Stir in cream cheese and cook until the cheese is melted completely.

3. Add milk and stir to blend.

4. Whisk in feta and mozzarella, lemon zest, dill, parsley, red pepper flakes, Greek yogurt, and lemon juice. Sprinkle some salt and pepper to taste and stir frequently for 5 minutes.

5. Transfer to a fondue pot and keep heat on low.

6. Garnish top with a drizzle of remaining oil, plus tomatoes and olives.

7. Serve with your pita chips platter.

# Smoky Mozzarella Fondue

Smoked mozzarella cheese is another twist that you can lend your fondue to make it as different as possible, not like what is usually served. It might not be the cheese variety that you are used to having but it is delicious alright, offering a wonderful base for various dipping ingredients, from breads to veggies to chips and cheese cubes.

**Serving Size:** 6

**Prep Time:** 30 mins

**Ingredients:**

- 1 cup smoked mozzarella cheese
- 8oz cream cheese, at room temperature
- 1 cup provolone cheese
- ½ cup Parmesan cheese, grated
- 1 pc tomato, chopped
- 1 tbsp parsley, chopped finely
- ½ tsp Italian seasoning
- ½ tsp dried thyme
- ¼ tsp red pepper flakes
- 1/3 cup sour cream
- Kosher salt and black pepper to taste

**Instructions:**

1. Preheat the oven to 350 degrees F.

2. Mix together the cheeses, sour cream, Italian seasoning, thyme, red pepper flakes, plus salt and pepper in a bowl until blended.

3. Transfer into a lightly greased baking pan and bake for 20 minutes. Broil for a few minutes to brown the top.

4. Serve with a garnish of chopped tomatoes and parsley in a fondue pot, together with your favorite dipping ingredients.

# Fiery Cheddar Fondue

Cheddar is a great choice of cheese to make into a fondue. In this recipe, the cheese fondue is made fiery with beer and fireball whiskey instead of just wine. What more can you ask for? It's a delightfully rich concoction perfect for dipping crusty bread cubes, broccoli florets, turnip and carrot strips, tortilla chips and whatever you imagine.

**Serving Size:** 12

**Prep Time:** 30 mins

**Ingredients:**

- 1 ½ cups white Cheddar cheese, grated
- 2 tbsp Fireball Whiskey
- 1 cup Lager-style beer
- 1 tbsp hot sauce
- 2 tbsp cornstarch
- 3 cups crusty bread cubes
- 4 cups vegetable mix

**Instructions:**

1. Combine cheese and cornstarch in a bowl. Set aside.

2. Heat beer in a pan over medium fire until slow boiling.

3. Gradually add cheese and cornstarch mix, stirring until melted with every addition.

4. Whisk in hot sauce and whiskey. Season with some salt and pepper and stir to blend until the mixture starts to bubble.

5. Serve in a fondue pot surrounded with bread cubes and different vegetables.

# Brie and Maple Syrup Fondue

Baked brie and maple syrup are the star of this fondue recipe. But you should not be afraid because the steps to getting closer to cheese heaven are not as complicated as they seem. They are in fact, simple enough to follow to get to the most delectable outcome your friends would certainly rave about.

**Serving Size:** 6

**Prep Time:** 20 mins

**Ingredients:**

- 8oz brie
- 3 tbsp maple syrup
- 3 pcs thyme sprigs
- 1 garlic clove, halved
- Pinch of salt
- 1 tbsp extra virgin olive oil
- 4 pcs garlic crostini, sliced
- ½ French stick sourdough, sliced

**Instructions:**

1. Preheat the oven to 375 degrees F. Arrange brie in a baking dish.

2. Pour in maple syrup on top. Then, sprinkle with thyme and a pinch of salt.

3. Bake brie in the oven for about 20 minutes. The center should feel soft to the touch.

4. Arrange bread slices in a serving platter and drizzle with olive oil.

5. Serve with baked brie. Cheese will ooze out as you make an opening.

# Pizza Fondue

This is pizza in a different dimension. Instead of having everything in one bite, the crust and the pizza sauce, loaded with cheese, of course, is served separately. But they are not to part. For this pizza fondue to be successful, you have to have that crusty bread available for dipping. Depending on your preference, you may also serve this fondue with veggies and chips. They would taste excellent, no matter what.

**Serving Size:** 6

**Prep Time:** 20 mins

**Ingredients:**

- 1-15oz jar marinara sauce
- 1-8oz package mini pepperoni slices
- 2 ½ cups mozzarella cheese, shredded
- 1/3 cup Parmesan cheese, grated
- ¼ tsp dried oregano
- 1 pc French baguette, sliced
- 1 cup tortilla chips

**Instructions:**

1. Place all the ingredients, except for baguette and chips, in a pan and heat over medium fire, stirring frequently until the cheeses melted.

2. Transfer into a fondue pot and keep warm on low heat.

3. Serve with chips and baguette slices.

# Mexican-Style Fondue

A festive fondue with a Mexican twang is something that you could serve on special occasions. It's a great addition to make a delightful buffet spread, especially since this fondue is deemed perfect for dipping veggies and chips and breads and what nots. Your certainly would love it.

**Serving Size:** 8

**Prep Time:** 1 hr. 45 mins

**Ingredients:**

- 1-16oz package processed cheese, cut into cubes
- 1-14.5oz diced tomatoes, drained
- 1-14.75oz can cream-style corn
- 3 tbsp green chilies, chopped
- 1 tsp chili powder
- 1 pc French bread loaf, cut into cubes
- 2 cups mixed vegetables (carrot strips, broccoli florets, turnips slices)

**Instructions:**

1. Combine all the ingredients, except for bread and mixed veggies, in a lightly greased slow cooker.

2. Cook for an hour and a half on high, stirring frequently, at least every half an hour, to melt cheese and keep the bottom from browning.

3. Transfer to a fondue pot and then keep warm on low heat. Serve with bread cubes and veggies.

# Spiced Oil Fondue

This is the authentic French-style fondue. It's just mostly oil, flavored with a couple of spices to provide a subtle effect into your taste buds. Apart from vegetables, you can also use meat as your dipping ingredient. You may also add bread into the equation to make a main course meal that you can serve to friends over a special, intimate dinner.

**Serving Size:** 6

**Prep Time:** 20 mins

**Ingredients:**

- ¾ cup olive oil
- 12 pcs anchovy fillets
- 6 garlic cloves, chopped
- 6 tbsp unsalted butter, at room temperature
- 3 cups assorted vegetables, cut into bite-size pieces
- 1 pc crusty French bread loaf, cut into 1-inch cubes
- 1 ½ cups skinless and boneless chicken breasts, cubed and boiled

**Instructions:**

1. Combine oil, anchovies, garlic, and butter in a food processor. Pulse until smooth.

2. Heat mixture in a pan over low fire, stirring occasionally for about 15 minutes.

3. Transfer into a fondue pot, keeping the oil temperature steady by putting a heat source on low.

4. Serve with vegetables, bread, and meat for dipping.

# Chinese Hot Pot

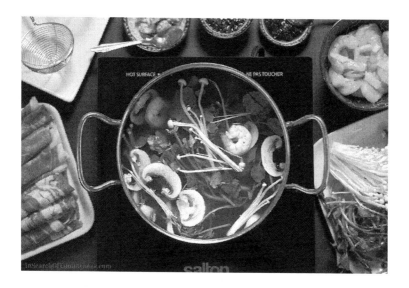

Nothing beats an elaborate Chinese Hot Pot to provide a full meal in a fondue party. This is the best choice if you are making the fondue your main course feature. It had been for years in many Asian countries (the Japanese has their own version of this fondue, which they call Shabu Shabu). To be successful at making the best hot pot, you must prepare a good broth. A tasty liquid could transform any piece of food into something extravagant. You can even use any leftover broth to create a one-bowl dish. Simply throw in some noodles along with your leftover meats and veggies.

**Serving Size:** 4

**Prep Time:** 15 mins

**Ingredients:**

- 3 cups beef broth
- 1 lb. sirloin beef, thinly sliced
- 4 pcs zucchini, sliced
- 2/3 cup Napa cabbage, sliced
- 2 pcs leeks, sliced
- 2 cups button mushrooms, sliced
- 3 ½ cups bean sprouts
- 1 ½ cups water

**For the Dipping Sauce:**

- ¼ cup soy sauce
- 3 tbsp lemon juice
- 5 tbsp sesame seeds, toasted and pounded

**Instructions:**

1. Combine water and beef broth in a pan and boil, stirring to blend.

2. Transfer to a fondue pot, keeping it constantly simmering on low heat.

3. Arrange the dipping ingredients in a serving platter.

4. To make the sauce, simply combine soy sauce and lemon juice with pounded sesame seeds.

5. Serve and enjoy.

# Swiss Tomato Fondue

Here is another classic Swiss fondue made extra delightful with tomatoes, garlic, and shallots. It stays true to the original fondue recipe but adds in some other ingredients to give it a twist. It's a great recipe for dipping not just breads but also fresh vegetables like carrots and radishes among many others.

**Serving Size:** 24

**Prep Time:** 40 mins

**Ingredients:**

- 1 lb. Gruyere cheese, grated
- 8oz Emmental cheese, grated
- 3 pcs tomatoes, seeded and chopped
- 2 garlic cloves, minced
- 1 pc shallot, minced
- 12oz dry white wine
- 2 tbsp butter

**Instructions:**

1. Melt butter in a pan over medium fire and sauté garlic and shallots until fragrant, about 5 minutes.

2. Stir in tomatoes and continue cooking for 3 minutes more.

3. Add wine and stir to blend until it comes to a soft boil.

4. Remove from heat, then, whisk in the cheeses, stirring until completely melted.

5. Transfer to a fondue pot and serve with your choice of dipping ingredients.

# Quick & Easy Chocolate Fondue

For ordinary foodies, there are only two types of fondue – one that is savory and another that is sweet. The sweet version usually comes in the form of chocolate, often served in a chocolate fountain to create an even stronger impact. Upon reading through this fondue cookbook, you will realize that you can actually tweak both versions with the addition of a few ingredients, or more. Cheese can be mixed with tomatoes, spices, and even meats to create a different concoction each time.

That is also true with the chocolate fondue. But for a good start, you must learn the basic recipe that will bring you a luscious, chocolatey fondue in under 10 minutes, using only two ingredients.

**Serving Size:** 4

**Prep Time:** 7 mins

**Ingredients:**

- 1 ½ cups chocolate chips
- 1-14oz can sweetened condensed milk

**Instructions:**

1. Mix together chocolates and milk in a pan and heat on low, stirring frequently until the chocolate has melted and the mixture becomes smooth.

2. Transfer chocolate fondue to a fondue pot or a chocolate fountain set.

3. Serve with your favorite dipping ingredients like marshmallows, crackers, cookies, and fresh fruits.

# Creamy Matcha Fondue

If you think the chocolate fondue is good enough, think again. There are countless twists that you can add to the basic recipe and make it extremely interesting. Otherwise, you may also bring together different ingredients to create a unique concoction that will play up in your taste buds. Try out matcha powder for a change. You won't regret it.

**Serving Size:** 4

**Prep Time:** 15 mins

**Ingredients:**

- 1 tsp cooking grade matcha powder
- 8oz white chocolate, chopped
- ½ cup heavy cream
- 1 cup pretzel rods
- 8 pcs mini muffins
- 1 cup marshmallows
- 1 cup fresh strawberries

**Instructions:**

1. Combine sifted matcha powder and a tablespoon of cream in a pan. Whisk until smooth.

2. Add white chocolates and remaining cream and heat over medium fire. Stir frequently until the chocolate is melted.

3. Transfer to a fondue pot and serve with your dipping ingredients.

4. Enjoy!

# Chocolate Cheesecake Fondue

Who says chocolate and cheese can't be together in one fondue pot? For this recipe, they can. Sweetened melted chocolate is made even more irresistible with the addition of cream cheese. It certainly pumps up the flavor.

**Serving Size:** 4

**Prep Time:** 20 mins

**Ingredients:**

- 2.5 oz of unsweetened baking chocolate, chopped finely
- 2 tbsp of Kahlua
- 2-16oz packages cream cheese, at room temperature
- ½ cup sugar

**Instructions:**

1. Heat cream cheese in a pan over medium fire until partially melted.

2. Stir in the dessert liqueur Kahlua and mix until blended.

3. Finally, add chopped chocolates and sugar and cook for another 5 minutes or more, stirring continuously until chocolates are melted and the sugar is dissolved.

4. Transfer to a fondue pot and serve with a platter of different dipping ingredients like fresh fruits, marshmallows, Graham crackers, brownies, and more.

# Caramel Fondue

Here's another easy, sweet concoction that you can whip up within 10 minutes. It's a great dipping sauce for a variety of treats, ranging from marshmallows to pretzels to brownies and cakes to crackers, and fruits. It's a truly delightful dish, a perfect backdrop for a truly satisfying meal, no matter what dipping ingredient you choose to dunk in.

**Serving Size:** 6

**Prep Time:** 10 mins

**Ingredients:**

- 25 pcs soft caramels
- ⅓ cup heavy cream
- ⅓ cup mini marshmallows
- ½ tsp fine salt

**Instructions:**

1. Combine all the ingredients, except for marshmallows, in a microwave safe bowl. Microwave for 3 minutes, stirring every minute to keep the consistency smooth.

2. Stir in marshmallows and return to the microwave for another minute.

3. Transfer to a fondue pot and then serve with your favorite dipping ingredients.

# Red Velvet Fondue

This Red Velvet Fondue is a great dessert idea for a romantic date for two. Whether it's your anniversary or a universal occasion such as Valentine's or even for no reason at all, it's worth going great lengths for putting together a delectable meal that you and your loved one would partake in That could easily make the night truly memorable.

**Serving Size:** 2

**Prep Time:** 25 mins

**Ingredients:**

- 1/3 cup heavy whipping cream
- 4oz milk chocolate, chopped
- 1 tbsp coffee liqueur
- 4 drops red food coloring
- 1 platter of cheesecake, biscuits, fruit and cake

**Instructions:**

1. Heat cream in a pan over medium fire.

2. Stir in chopped chocolates and coffee liqueur. Mix until completely melted.

3. Transfer to a fondue pot heated on low and serve with a platter of treats for dipping.

# Cinnamon Roll Fondue

This is party food at its finest! It's a simple cream cheese dipping sauce that is best served with cinnamon rolls. You can add other treats as your dipping ingredients, like one-day old cakes, brownies, cookies, mallows, crackers, and bread sticks. The flavor is just oh-so-yummy. Perfect to perk up your mood instantly.

**Serving Size:** 6

**Prep Time:** 2 hrs. 20 mins

**Ingredients:**

- 1-8oz package cream cheese, at room temperature
- Pinch of cinnamon
- 2 cups powdered sugar
- ½ cup butter, at room temperature
- 1 ½ tsp vanilla extract

**Instructions:**

1. Combine cream cheese, cinnamon, butter, and vanilla in a mixer. Beat until smooth.

2. Gradually add sugar and mix until well combined.

3. Transfer mixture in a slow cooker and cook on low for an hour and a half, stirring occasionally.

4. Pour fondue in a fondue pot and heat on low to keep it warm.

5. Serve with bite-size cinnamon rolls and other treats.

# S'mores Fondue

S'mores sound so good, no matter which way you have it. What's more if it comes in fondue form so you can dunk in delectable treats to make them even more of an indulgence? This is the perfect comfort food. It will surely lighten up your mood.

**Serving Size:** 2

**Prep Time:** 10 mins

**Ingredients:**

- 2 cups mini marshmallows
- 1 ½ cup marshmallow crème
- 24oz milk chocolate, broken into smaller pieces
- 1/3 cup heavy cream
- ¼ cup graham crackers, crumbled
- 1 platter of Graham crackers, strawberries, and marshmallows

**Instructions:**

1. Heat marshmallow crème, heavy cream, and chocolates in a pan over medium fire. Stir frequently until smooth and melty.

2. Meanwhile, broil marshmallows for a couple of minutes.

3. Add half of broiled mallows into the fondue, reserving the others for topping. Stir until creamy.

4. Transfer fondue into a fondue pot, garnish with crumbled Grahams and broiled marshmallows, and serve with your dipping ingredients.

# Butterscotch Fondue

Butterscotch seems like a nice fondue flavor. Don't you think so? Try this recipe and discover how you can make butterscotch as a wonderful background for an extremely appetizing dessert that you and your friends could partake in.

**Serving Size:** 4

**Prep Time:** 3 hrs. 10 mins

**Ingredients:**

- 1-14oz can sweetened condensed milk
- ½ cup unsalted butter, melted
- 1/3 cup light corn syrup
- 1 cup brown sugar
- 1/8 cup milk
- ½ tsp vanilla extract

**Instructions:**

1. Pour all the ingredients in a slow cooker and cook for 3 hours on low. Stir occasionally.

2. Transfer to a fondue pot and serve with an assortment of fruits, cakes, and crackers for dipping.

# Lemon Fondue

Adding lemon flavor into a fondue is quite smart. It will give the dish a balanced taste. If you are not a fan of too much sweetness, this kind of dessert would be ideal. It's perfect to prepare for special luncheons and keep tongues a-wagging.

**Serving Size:** 10

**Prep Time:** 15 mins

**Ingredients:**

- ½ cup lemon juice
- 2 tbsp lemon zest, grated
- ½ cup butter, cubed
- 1 cup sugar
- ½ cup cornstarch
- ½ tsp salt
- 4 cups water

**Instructions:**

1. Combine cornstarch, sugar, salt, and water in a pan. Heat on medium fire and stir to blend.

2. When the solids are dissolved, turn off heat.

3. Whisk in the remaining ingredients until the butter is completely melted and the consistency is smooth.

4. Place butterscotch concoction in a fondue pot and serve with your favorite dipping ingredients.

# Mocha Fondue

The thing with fondues is that, you have endless opportunities to have fun with different ingredients and what to dip in it. As long as you have a nice base, which is the fondue, you can pick any food morsel that you want to significantly enhance its taste and satisfaction level. This Mocha Fondue is one of the most wonderful bases that you can serve for dessert to ensure that your guests will have a lot of fun dipping in pieces of bread, cakes, and fruits.

**Serving Size:** 4

**Prep Time:** 20 mins

**Ingredients:**

- 3 cups milk chocolate chips
- 1 tbsp instant coffee granules, dissolved in
- 2 tbsp hot water
- ½ cup heavy whipping cream
- 1/8 tsp ground cinnamon
- 1 tsp vanilla extract
- 1 pc pound cake, cubed
- 2 cups fresh fruits (strawberries, kiwi, grapes, or cherries)

**Instructions:**

1. Melt chocolate chips together with whipping cream in a pan over medium fire.

2. Stir in coffee and water mixture, cinnamon, and vanilla. Mix to blend.

3. Transfer to a fondue pot and serve with cake cubes and bite-size fruits.

# Conclusion

Everybody loves to fondue. It is easy to see why. This cuisine specialty is popular across different regions because they can easily tweak the recipe to fit it into their own taste.

A fondue is no longer just about the Swiss cheese fondue, which is an integral part of the world food culture. It can be made with different ingredients and into different blends to fit into what is required at the dining table. It is no longer just about a meal starter. This appetizing dish can be upgraded to a main course meal and even turned into a dessert.

From cheese to chocolate to meat broth and spiced oils, you can make different fondue recipes for all occasions, depending on what the event is, what you are dipping, and what your taste buds prefer. And oh, you should never forget that fondue is a communal dish that is meant to be shared. Do not fondue on your own. Take the fun level a few notches higher by calling in friends and family members to dunk in and enjoy!

Happy cooking!

**Dear Reader,**

Thank you very much for choosing my book. I hope you really enjoy it. If don't mind I would like to ask you to leave a review after reading.

Thanks.

Sincerely yours,

Stephanie Sharp

Made in the USA
San Bernardino, CA
13 December 2019